Contents

1. Who is the Holy Spirit? — 1
2. What is the Indwelling of the Holy Spirit? — 6
3. The Human Soul, the Human Spirit, and the Holy Spirit — 10
4. Cultivating a Mind Like Christ's — 16
5. The Battle for the Mind — 21
6. The Disordered Mind — 26
7. Living with the Advantage — 30
8. Works Cited — 35

Websites — 36

Section I

WHO IS THE HOLY SPIRIT?

Questions to Consider

- What thoughts, understanding, or church culture experiences do you have about the Holy Spirit?
- What have you heard or thought about what the Holy Spirit might look like or how the Holy Spirit interacts with us?

The Holy Spirit is mentioned over eighty times in the Old Testament and over 250 times in the New Testament. In this section you will learn the essential character and personhood of the Holy Spirit.

The Holy Spirit is the most disregarded entity in the Godhead. The Holy Spirit is the same spirit that hovered over the earth with God in the beginning. Genesis 1:1-2, ***In the beginning God created the heavens and the earth.*** *²* ***The earth was formless and empty, and darkness covered the deep waters. And the Spirit of God was hovering over the surface of the waters.*** The Holy Spirit was in the beginning with God and is God. He is also known in the New Testament as the "Spirit of Christ." 1 Peter 1:10-1, ***This salvation was something even the prophets wanted to know more about when*** *they prophesied about this gracious salvation prepared for you. ¹¹ They wondered what time or situation the Spirit of Christ within them was talking about when he told them in advance about Christ's suffering and his great glory afterward.*

The Holy Spirit is not some sort of cosmic force that gets on you, but the Holy Spirit is a person because the Holy Spirit has personality. The Holy Spirit is God. John 14:26, *But when the Father sends the Advocate as my representative—that is, the Holy Spirit—he will teach you everything and will remind you of everything I have told you.* Also, John 16:13, *When the Spirit of truth comes, he will guide you into all truth. He will not speak on his own but will tell you what he has heard. He will tell you about the future.*

Proof of the Holy Spirit's personhood is:

The Holy Spirit can be blasphemed (Matthew 12:31-32).

So, I tell you, every sin and blasphemy can be forgiven—except blasphemy against the Holy Spirit, which will never be forgiven. Anyone who speaks against the Son of Man can be forgiven, but anyone who speaks against the Holy Spirit will never be forgiven, either in this world or in the world to come.

The Holy Spirit can be insulted (Hebrews 10:29).

Just think how much worse the punishment will be for those who have trampled on the Son of God, and have treated the blood of the covenant, which made us holy, as if it were common and unholy, and have insulted and disdained the Holy Spirit who brings God's mercy to us.

The Holy Spirit can be grieved (Ephesians 4:30).

And do not bring sorrow to God's Holy Spirit by the way you live. Remember, he has identified you as his own, guaranteeing that you will be saved on the day of redemption.

The Holy Spirit can be lied to (Acts 5:3)

Then Peter said, "Ananias, why have you let Satan fill your heart? You lied to the Holy Spirit, and you kept some of the money for yourself.

The Holy Spirit can be resisted (Acts 7:51)

You stubborn people! You are heathen at heart and deaf to the truth. Must you forever resist the Holy Spirit? That is what your ancestors did, and so do you!

The Holy Spirit has wisdom and intelligence (1 Corinthians 2:11)

No one can know a person's thoughts except that person's own spirit, and no one can know God's thoughts except God's own Spirit.

The Holy Spirit speaks with a will and authority (Acts 13:2).

One day as these men were worshiping the Lord and fasting, the Holy Spirit said, "Appoint Barnabas and Saul for the special work to which I have called them."

The Holy Spirit radiates goodness (Psalm 143:10)

Teach me to do your will, for you are my God.
May your gracious Spirit lead me forward on a firm footing.

The Holy Spirit shares in fellowship (2 Corinthians 13:14)

May the grace of the Lord Jesus Christ, the love of God, and the fellowship of the Holy Spirit be with you all.

The Holy Spirit shares God's attributes and does what only God can do. The Holy Spirit is God, God in us. Whatever God can do, the Holy Spirit can do. The Holy Spirit was in the beginning with God and is the power behind the inspiration of prophecy and scriptures (2 Timothy 3:15).

The following chart identifies attributes of God and attributes of the Holy Spirit.

Qualities and Abilities of Deity	Attributed to God	Attributed to the Holy Spirit
Omnipresence Being in all places at the same time.	Jeremiah 23:23-24 Acts 17:24-28	Psalm 139:7-12
Omniscience Knowledge of all that can be known.	Hebrews 4:13 1 John 3:20	1 Corinthians 2:10-11
Omnipotence The power over all physical and spiritual beings.	Genesis 28:3; 35:11 1 Chronicles 29:10-13	Romans 15:19

Creation	Genesis 1:1 Ephesians 3:9	Genesis 1:2 Psalm 104:30
Providence	1 Timothy 6:17	Romans 8:26-28
Power of Resurrection	1 Kings 17:21-22 Romans 6:4	Romans 8:11
Sanctification	1 Thessalonians 5:23	2 Thessalonians 2:13
Revelation of God's Will	Matthew 11:25 2 Timothy 3:16	John 3:5 1 Corinthians 2:10
Eternal	Deuteronomy 33:27	Hebrews 9:14

(*Clouded by Emotion*, Lance Moser, page 8)

Prayer

Welcome Holy Spirit. Thank you for the revelation of who you really are. I invite you in my life. May I become more aware of your Presence in me. Baptize me with the fire of Your Love and the peace of your Presence. My life flows from you. You are my breath. Guide me so that my life may become a fruitful offering to You. Come Holy Spirit. Come.

Section II
What is the Indwelling of the Holy Spirit?

Questions to Consider

- What does it mean to indwell?
- When does the Holy Spirit indwell a person?
- What blessing does the indwelling of the Holy Spirit provide?
- What does it mean to be filled with the Holy Spirit?

When a person has believed, repented of sin, and confessed Christ as Savior, that person is sealed with the Holy Spirit. You will learn what it means to have the abiding presence or indwelling of the Holy Spirit as you engage in this section.

When a person believes in Christ, they are "born again." That means that they are renewed (regenerated) spiritually and are no longer in their previous state of being separated from God. They are in a new state of being a "child of God." This is what it means to be indwelled by the Holy Spirit.

John 1:12-13
Yet to all who did receive him, to those who believed in his name, he gave the right to become children of God— ¹³ children born not of natural descent, nor of human decision or a husband's will, but born of God.

Most of the New Testament is written to teach you how to live by the Spirit because the Holy Spirit is given to the believer as a promise of inheritance. Your salvation is a three-prong process:

- You are saved from the penalty of sin.
- You are being saved from the power of sin.
- You will be saved from the presence of sin.

This is called sanctification.

Read Romans 8. In this chapter you will learn that the indwelling Spirit gives life to your spirit. The Holy Spirit gives life where there was death and gives peace where there was hostility. Your repentance and baptism raise you to a newness of life and allow you to be born again to a living hope (Romans 8:14-17).

One of the blessings that is provided through the indwelling of the Holy Spirit is the ability to communicate with God, the Father – even if you do not know what to say. The Spirit helps you by interceding on your behalf (Romans 8:26-27). Another blessing of the Holy Spirit is that you and the entire church are temples where the Holy Spirit dwells (see Ephesians 2:19-21; 1 Timothy 3:14-15; and 1 Peter 2:4-10).

When you consider the role of the temple in the Old Testament, it was the habitation of God. It was the place where God dwelled, and it was the place where Jewish believers fellowshipped with God and one another. It was also the place of sacrifice, where one could seek forgiveness, a place of prayer and where the glory of God was housed.

Before the death of Christ there was a separation between God and humankind. We could not approach God directly. Since the death of Christ, the hostility that separated God and humanity was done away with. Now, because of the Holy Spirit, we have direct access to God. The church is no longer just a geographical location. We have become the church because we carry the presence of the Holy Spirit. Church is translated from the Greek as "ekklesia" meaning the called-out ones. The Holy Spirit in us makes God's presence available to us at will. Now the church is no longer just a place, but it is a people. We have been made alive in Christ and are living stones (see 1 Peter 2:4-5).

Because you have believed in Christ, God's Spirit is active in your life and provides you many blessings. You have a "down payment on your ultimate salvation, spiritual life, confirmation of adoption as a child of God, help in prayer, and fellowship with God and his people (see Ephesians 1:3).

So then, if the Holy Spirit lives in you, you can walk in the Spirit (Galatians 5:18). When believers allow the word of God to dwell richly in them (Colossians 3:16), they are open and receptive to the influence of the Holy Spirit and allow the Word and the Holy Spirit to shape their lives. They begin to look a lot like Jesus. Love, joy, peace, forbearance, kindness, goodness, faithfulness, gentleness, and self-control begin to order their days. In other words, they will begin to bear the fruit of the Spirit.

Prayer

Holy Spirit, Comforter and Friend, let our hearts be your habitation. As I give myself to you, dwell richly in me that I might honor you and not grieve you. Fill me with your compassionate love. Watch over me in weakness. Be my help in my infirmity and keep me by your grace.

Section III

THE HUMAN SOUL, THE HUMAN SPIRIT, AND THE HOLY SPIRIT

Questions to Consider

- How does the human spirit differ from the human soul?
- Describe the characteristics of the soulish life?
- How can you apply "walking in the Spirit" to help you navigate day-to-day challenges?
- How can you distinguish between the voice of the soul and the voice of the spirit?

Often believers use soul and spirit interchangeably. However, they each have distinct qualities. Understanding the distinction between your soul and spirit will help you see the work of the Holy Spirit more clearly. Section III will help you distinguish between each of them.

The Holy Spirit

The Holy Spirit is with you and willing to engage with you every day if allowed. It is up to you to learn to become conscious of His presence and invite His participation. You must be an active participant in what the Holy Spirit wants to do in your life on earth.

Humankind can commune with God because of the Holy Spirit. However, if you do not have the ability to recognize your own spirit, then you have no knowledge of how to commune with God. You will be led by your own thoughts and emotions and falsely believe it is the work of the Holy Spirit. You will be a prisoner of the soul.

> **1Corinthians 2:11, NIV**
> **For who knows a person's thoughts except their own spirit within them? In the same way no one knows the thoughts of God except the Spirit of God.**
>
> **Proverbs 25:28, NKJV**
> **Whoever *has* no rule over his own spirit**
> ***Is like* a city broken down, without walls.**

Human beings possess a human spirit. It is different from the soul or the Holy Spirit. We worship God in our human spirit (John 4:24).

The human spirit has three main functions – conscience, intuition, and fellowship:

- Your **conscience** allows you to discern what is right and wrong. It is a spontaneous and direct judgment. It is that which raises the voice of accusation in you when you do wrong.
- **Intuition** is a directing inner sense that has no outside influence. You know through your intuition and understand with your mind. You experience revelation of and from God and the movement of the Holy Spirit through intuition.

Believers must pay attention to the voice of the conscience, and the leading of intuition.

- **Communion** is how you fellowship with and worship God. You cannot grasp or perceive God in your thoughts, feelings, or intentions. God can only be known in the human spirit. The human spirit is what Paul refers to as the "inner man".

The spirit contains the function of conscience (discernment), the function of intuition (spiritual sense) and the function of communion (worship).

This chart gives additional scriptural references for greater clarity about the three elements of the human spirit.

Conscience	Intuition	Communion
Psalm 51:10	Acts 18:25, 1 Cor. 2:11	Luke 1:47, Romans 8:16

The Soul

Aside from having a spirit, you also possess a soul. You are made conscious of your existence through the soul. All that makes you human belongs to the soul. It is the seat of personality – intellect, thought, ideals, love, emotion, discernment, choice, and decisions. Because the soul houses the personality, sometimes you will see humans referred to as souls in the Bible (Gen. 12:5, Gen. 46:27).

Your personality is made up of three main abilities: the will, the mind, and emotions:

- Your **will** is your power to choose.
- Your **mind** manifests your intellectual power – wisdom, knowledge, and reasoning.
- Your **emotions** enable you to express what you like or dislike. You can express love or hate, joy, anger, sadness, and happiness. Without emotions, you would be like statues, cold and unfeeling.

There are two Greek words for life that I want to introduce -- psuché and zoé. **Psuché** is the soul life, the animated life of humanity, the natural life. Your natural life is a composite of your mind, intellect, emotions, and will. **Zoé** is the highest form of life. It is the spiritual life. Psuché and Zoé are important because they distinguish what type of Christian life you live -- soulish or spiritual. A soulish life is a life led by emotions and feelings. A spiritual life is a life surrendered to and led by the Holy Spirit.

The chart below offers a comparison of the soulish life versus the spiritual life.

*The Spiritual Life

Soulish Life (Psuché)	Spiritual Life (Zoé)
A crisis	A continual process
Based on knowledge	Based on obedience
External	Internal
Automatic	Cultivated

Produced by [your] energy	Produced by divine enablement
A dream	A discipline
An unusual experience	A normal experience
A list of rules	A life of relationship
To be endured	To be enjoyed
Theoretical	Intensely practical

*Adapted from Conformed to His Image, Kenneth Boa

The spiritual life is the "life of Christ reproduced in the believer by the power of the Holy Spirit in obedient response to the Word of God". This is the reality of your new identity as you learn through experience:

- Your freedom from the law of sin and of death through the Spirit of life in Christ Jesus (Romans 8:2). The key to your freedom from the power of sin is your co-crucifixion with Christ and the indwelling power of the Spirit. You are no longer under the law but under grace (Romans 6:14).
- Your brokenness or realizing the bankruptcy of your own resources and effort along with your unconditional surrender are part of the process of appropriating Christ as life (Romans 7:14-25; 12:1-2; 2 Corinthians 12:9-10; Galatians 5:24).
- The spiritual life is an inside-out rather than an outside-in process (Ephesians 3:16-19).
- The exchanged life is not a matter of trying to do things for Jesus but of claiming and resting in what He has already

done for you (Galatians 2:20). The new nature you now possess in Him is now your deepest identity, and the *practice* of sin is incompatible with the new creation you have become as a child of God (2 Corinthians 5:17; 1 John 2:1-2; 3:1-10). While you are in this body, you will experience the pull of the old beliefs, attitudes, and dispositions, but you must see yourself as a new person, adopted into God's family, who need not yield to the lures of the flesh (Romans 8:12-17).

Prayer

Holy Spirit, teach me to pray in the Spirit. Help me to wield the sword of the Spirit which is the word of God to take authority over the murmurings of my soul. Your perfect love casts out fear. Holy Spirit, you are not the voice of confusion and condemnation but of conviction and correction. In Your perfect love, instruct me in Your ways. In Jesus' name, Amen.

Section IV

CULTIVATING A MIND LIKE CHRIST'S

Questions to Consider

- What does it mean to have a mind of like Christ?
- How does thinking more like Christ compare to adopting the thinking of the culture?
- It is hard to know who or what to believe when we live in a world where "everything is relevant." What unwavering truth do you stand on?
- Do you tend to be more "soulish" or more "spiritual"?

While you are a free agent in every respect, you have the ability to cultivate a mind like Christ and transform your thinking. You will learn how to apply this truth in this section so that you do not have to be ruled by your emotions.

God created humans to be free thinking agents. God had no desire to force people to follow Him or to control their behavior. He desires that humanity might follow Him freely of their own will. God promises that when you surrender your life to His will, He will direct your path.

You must choose every day between the ways of God (walking in the Spirit) and the ways of the culture (soulish responses). You cannot choose God's ways apart from knowing the Word and partnering with the Holy Spirit. Your studies are not just to learn information but to discover God's transforming power by meditating on His word. When you partner with the Holy Spirit, you invite Him into your day or your circumstances and allow Him to lead. By doing this your mind is renewed, and you begin to be transformed. As your thinking is being changed, your attitudes and behaviors will begin to change.

Cultivating a mind like Christ's is not something you can achieve on your own; it is primarily the work of the Holy Spirit. When you surrender your will to God's, the Holy Spirit will complete the work that God began in you.

Philippians 2:13
for it is God who works in you to will and to act in order to fulfill his good purpose.

Humanity is made in the image of God. You see in scripture that God experiences emotions such as grief, anger, and wrath. Likewise, you also experience a range of emotions. Without emotions, you would be like a robot walking around without feeling.

Emotions are good. Every one of them. God gave them to you, but you cannot cultivate a mind like Christ's without learning to manage them. Emotions are essential to human experience and can influence how you think and behave. Every day your emotions can influence the decisions you make and the actions you take, both great and small. They can be fleeting or lasting and can fluctuate in a moment. Emotions can drive how you experience the world and how you express yourself. They can show up in your body and can affect your health. Worry, stress, and depression can lead to many sicknesses: high blood pressure, ulcers, headaches, weight loss or gain, insomnia, and unexplained pain.

Your emotions are important and should not be ignored. It is important to know how you feel. Sometimes, you just need to sit with your emotions, whatever they may be. Whether it is grief, anger, or sadness, you need to feel all that the emotions bring before you can heal or move forward. Likewise, on the contrary, you need to savor times of joy, happiness, and delight and embed them deep into your memory.

It is unhealthy to ignore emotions, but it is also spiritually unwise to allow yourself to be ruled by them. Often, God will use your emotions to reveal your heart because your heart is deceptive (Jeremiah 19:9). For example, you may believe you have forgiven someone, but the sight of that person is gut-wrenching and stirs up anger. That response can cause you to realize that you haven't forgiven them completely. Dealing with your emotions in a godly way is necessary for spiritual growth. You must be fully in touch with your feelings and then integrate them with the word of God. For example, never call what is right wrong or justify your wrong behaviors. If you do, it will begin to harden your heart, and you will lose your ability to be sensitive to the things of God.

There are cultural ideas about emotions that influence the development of men and women. Men are most often taught to suppress emotions. Women are often encouraged to experience their emotions but also can be penalized for doing so. With the guidance of the Holy Spirit everyone can develop a healthy emotional self to better equip them in moving toward a relationship with the Holy Spirit.

There are different schools of thought concerning emotions. Some experts believe that you simply feel what you feel, and it cannot be changed. They believe what you feel controls your responses. Other experts believe that you can choose how you react in spite of how you are feeling. God's word implies that you can choose your emotional responses and control your behaviors. With the help of the Holy Spirit, you can choose how to respond to any situation regardless of the emotions you are experiencing.

Proverbs 16:32
Better a patient person than a warrior,
one with self-control than one who takes a city.

Galatians 5:16-18, 22-24
So I say, walk by the Spirit, and you will not gratify the desires of the flesh. For the flesh desires what is contrary to the Spirit, and the Spirit what is contrary to the flesh. They are in conflict with each other, so that you are not to do

whatever you want. But if you are led by the Spirit, you are not under the law.

But the fruit of the Spirit is love, joy, peace, forbearance, kindness, goodness, faithfulness, gentleness and self-control. Against such things there is no law. Those who belong to Christ Jesus have crucified the flesh with its passions and desires.

To promote the growth and development necessary to think more like Christ, you must spend time in prayer, study, and mediation on God's word. It may seem overwhelming or for some it may even seem frightening, but it's not something you have to accomplish on your own. It is primarily the work of the Holy Spirit. All you must do is surrender your will, become a partner in the process, and allow the Holy Spirit to complete what He has already begun in you.

Prayer

Holy Spirit, I thank you for helping me to develop a mind like Christ. I give you permission to transform the way I think as I feed myself your Word. Fill me with wisdom, knowledge, and understanding so that I am able to walk in the Spirit and reflect Christ in the world. I thank you that because Christ has overcome the world, I have also, and I am free from fear, doubt, confusion, and doublemindedness. Amen.

Section V

THE BATTLE FOR THE MIND

Questions to Consider

- What is a stronghold and how are they developed?
- What is the difference between a stronghold and a sin?
- What spiritual weapons help to dismantle strongholds?
- What does it mean to be carnally minded?

You are in battle every day with a real enemy. Satan wages war against the children of God and the battle is for the mind. Here you will learn three key areas that the enemy uses to attack your thinking and how to overcome Satan's attacks.

Since your behavior begins with a thought, the mind is the most potent battlefield because it is the center and source of your actions. In this section, you will focus on the strongholds that can lead you away from God and steal your joy. You will learn more about overcoming the strongholds that hinder you from living the abundant life that Jesus promised. John 10:10 says, "**The thief comes only to steal and kill and destroy; I have come that they may have life and have it to the full**".

There is a difference between sin and strongholds. A sin is an act of willful disobedience to the revealed will of God. However, strongholds are harmful thought patterns, arrogant attitudes, or messages from the culture that have left a lasting impression on the believer's heart and mind. They are so deeply rooted that you often think of them as just who you are or a part of your personality and don't recognize that they are in opposition to God. Strongholds often begin in childhood and can be carried through adulthood. Strongholds can be influenced by an emotional response to a circumstance or situation. Here are three common examples of how strongholds are created.

1. **LIES YOU HAVE BELIEVED:** These include lies about God, about yourself, and lies about how God sees you. They are lies that the enemy has been playing over and over in your mind for years, which, in your pain, you've unfortunately bought into. For example, many men and women grow up with body issues surrounding weight, skin color, or hair. This can cause feelings of shame and inadequacy. The truth is that we are all fearfully (with reverence) and wonderfully made in the image of God.

2. **A PUNATIVE GOD:** Some of you may have grown up with an image of a punitive God, waiting to punish every misdeed. As a result, you have become afraid of God.

3. **THE INABILITY TO FORGIVE:** You may still be nursing bitterness against someone who has wronged you. If so, the enemy will take advantage of that to keep you in

bondage. You may not feel that those who have wounded you should be forgiven, but we forgive because Jesus Christ forgave us for an even greater sin against God. We also forgive because it sets us free from the bondage produced by bitterness. Some people believe that they cannot forgive someone unless they receive an apology, but the truth is we are to forgive because we have been forgiven.

4. **HEREDITARY PATTERNS IN YOUR LINEAGE:** You may have noticed the fact that certain unhealthy behavioral and thought patterns present in your life were also present in your father's (or mother's) life, and his father's, and so on. Sometimes unhealthy, even ungodly family traditions and family patterns are passed down from generation to generation to generation until someone stands up and proclaims, IN JESUS' NAME, NO MORE! For example, for some getting counseling to help address difficult moments in life is seen as taboo, but the Bible says that he who seeks counsel is wise (Proverbs 12:15). Another example would be accumulating debt because there is a lack of disciplined financial management.

To overcome these (and other) similar patterns, you must submit yourself to the leading of the Holy Spirit by elevating into the thinking of Christ and commit to the practical steps needed to overcome the bondage.

2 Corinthians 10:3-5
For though we live in the world, we do not wage war as the world does. ⁴The weapons we fight with are not the weapons of the world. On the contrary, they have divine power to demolish strongholds. We demolish arguments and every pretension that sets itself up against the knowledge of God, and we take captive every thought to make it obedient to Christ.

If you do not guard your thoughts and become intentional about shifting your negative thinking, and if you do not become certain of your identity in Christ, you will be tossed and driven by your emotions and every ear tickling (feel good) doctrine you may hear. In the modern global context, you must have some level of emotional and spiritual stability. If not, you will be prone to fear, anxiety, stress, worry, and depression.

With the weapons of your warfare, you can (1) take every thought captive, (2) cast down thinking that contradicts God's word, (3) cast down imaginations (continuous worst-case thinking), and (4) pull down strongholds. When you are overcome with vain imaginations, and negative thinking, you can negate them by remembering the truth of God's word that counteracts or contradicts their purpose. You are to put on the "helmet of salvation" that guards your mind. **Take the helmet of salvation and the sword of the Spirit, which is the word of God** (Ephesians 6:17).

Remember, whatever you feed will grow. Thoughts are seeds. Meditating or ruminating on those thoughts water the seeds and cause them to grow. The resulting behavior associated with the seeds (thinking) is the fruit (behavior). To cultivate a mind like Christ you must take control of your thoughts by understanding that,

- Your mind is yours. You have free will and can control your thoughts.
- You must judge your thoughts and align them with scripture.
- You must consistently speak the word of God into your own mind. Affirm each day what God says is true concerning every area of your life.

Proverbs 12:18, **The words of the reckless pierce like swords, but the tongue of the wise brings healing.** You must decide to speak the word of God into your life and to receive or reject what people say because people have the power to bless you or hurt you.

Prayer

Holy Spirit, I pray that you will bring to mind every stronghold in my life. I ask that you give me the courage to cast away those lies that I elevate over the truth of your Word. Help me to use your Word to pull down every stronghold. I give you permission to change me. In Jesus' name. Amen.

Section VI

THE DISORDERED MIND

Questions to Consider

- When have you experienced a time when your motive, speech or actions were not aligned?
- Have you ever had to interact regularly with a double-minded person? What was that experience like?
- What does it mean to have freedom in Christ?
- What steps can be taken to develop an ordered mind?

The disordered mind rejects the will of God. The result of being led by emotions and not submitting to the will of God is instability and doublemindedness.

A disordered mind in scripture is known as doublemindedness. It comes from the Greek *dispsuchos*, which means a person with two minds or two souls. It is used only in the book of James (James 1:8, 4:8). James describes doubleminded people as "unstable in all their ways". This is what Jesus had in mind when He spoke of those who try to serve two masters (Matthew 6:24).

Disordered thinking causes restlessness and confusion in thought, speech, and actions. If your thinking is disordered, your biggest conflict is within you, but disordered thinking can also put you in conflict with other people and God. If your thinking is disordered, your mind has no direction. Like a lost hiker in the woods, you aimlessly follow one wrong path after another. That is why believers are instructed to let "your yes be yes, and your no be no" (Matthew 5:37).

Although doubleminded people may have great knowledge, they lack the faith that moves the heart of God. *Faith shows the reality of what we hope for; it is the evidence of things we cannot see.* In Hebrews 11 you learn that you cannot have faith and doubt at the same time. In order to access and walk in the mind of Christ, you must believe that you are a new creation in Christ. *This means that anyone who belongs to Christ has become a new person. The old life is gone; a new life has begun!* 2 Corinthians 5:17.

According to James 4:1, the reason believers have mental conflicts and battles is because of the desires that battle within them. **What causes fights and quarrels among you? Don't they come from your desires that battle within you?** When your desires are in conflict and you are led by your emotions, you have a disordered mind. Spiritually speaking, a disordered mind is when your will is in direct conflict with God's revealed will. It is when the mind is dominated by the flesh. **The mind governed by the flesh is hostile to God; it does not submit to God's law, nor can it do so** (Romans 8:7).

When you are led by your emotions, you rely too much on your feelings and not enough on the truth of God's word. Feelings are unreliable. Your feelings can change from moment to moment, and you can find yourself on an emotional rollercoaster ride that robs you of your peace and joy.

There are many ways that emotions can control you. For example, ruminating on anger can lead to resentment. Lashing out can cause you to harm someone emotionally and physically. Infatuation can lead to a premature relationship. Pride can lead to alienating others and a false sense of confidence. Fear can lead to anxiety and worry. Each of these emotions can be difficult to re-direct on your own. If allowed, they can dominate your behavior and hold you hostage. The result is uncontrollable, impulsive behavior.

God's desire is that you have freedom; that you be free from the negative mindset of the world. When you consider the Exodus story (Exodus 1-19), God wanted to free Israel not only from slavery, but from the system of oppression. He wanted not only their bodies to be free, but their minds to be free as well. Why? So that the Israelites could worship Him!

Oppression is prolonged, unjust treatment or control or the feeling of being heavily burdened -- mentally or physically -- by troubles, adverse conditions, or anxiety. We live in a world that is brimming with oppression. Not only is there gender, racial, and religious oppression, but there is political oppression, and corporate exploitation. You may also have personal circumstances that oppress you, such as unresolved grief, sickness, financial challenges, or troubled children.

We also live in a world with an ever-changing political landscape. There is also an escalation of violence and lawlessness. There are wars and rumors of wars. The economy is often unpredictable. Chaos and confusion are the order of the day. Yet even during personal challenges and the chaos of the world, God wants you to be free from oppression and worship Him. How can you do that? By relying on the Holy Spirit. The Holy Spirit is our comforter, keeper, advocate, and friend. With the Holy Spirit, you have the advantage.

Prayer

Lord, I confess that I have often been double-minded. I have tried to navigate life with my own efforts and have used the patterns of the world as my guide. I am grateful that your love, grace, and mercy have sustained me. I understand that my ways are not your ways, and neither are your thoughts my thoughts. Today, I choose to submit myself to you and the truth of your word. Help me, Holy Spirit. Amen.

Section VII

LIVING WITH THE ADVANTAGE

Questions to Consider

- Read John 16. What advantage does the Holy Spirit give believers?
- The Holy Spirit gives us an advantage over our weaknesses. What areas of your life or thinking do you need to yield to the Holy Spirit?
- What is wisdom? How does the Holy Spirit make you wise?

This final section examines the victorious life that you can live in Christ when actively in fellowship with the Holy Spirit. It proves that life with the Holy Spirit is a life that brings freedom, peace, and purpose.

The book of Philippians is a personal and passionate letter that Paul wrote from prison under the threat of execution. One of the things he emphasizes is the joy that life in Christ brings to all believers in all circumstances, good and bad.

> **Philippians 4:8-9**
> **Finally, brothers and sisters, whatever is true, whatever is noble, whatever is right, whatever is pure, whatever is lovely, whatever is admirable—if anything is excellent or praiseworthy—think about such things. Whatever you have learned or received or heard from me or seen in me, put it into practice. And the God of peace will be with you.**

How was Paul able to have the peace of God although he faced execution? He stood resolutely on his identity in Christ, the hope of the resurrection, and took authority over his thought life by walking in the Spirit. At this point in his life Paul experienced hunger, isolation, and persecution. However, he also experienced a life of abundance with the affirmation of the church and support of friends. Having experienced both extremes, Paul learned to be content in every situation and circumstance he found himself, and you can too.

Believers are created for victory. However, you can't achieve it alone. To walk in victory, you must be in fellowship and partnership with the Holy Spirit. You must walk in the Holy Spirit. You must persist in doing what you know leads to freedom from emotional bondage and confusion. The only reason believers can't be free is because they won't commit to God's process.

When the problems of emotional overload and negative thinking arise – and they most definitely will – you must be willing to apply the Biblical methods for freedom and deliverance. You must order your thinking and take on the mind of Christ. You can surrender to the enemy and believe, "That's just the way I am. I always worry just like my mom does. Anxiety runs in our family." If you do, you will remain in bondage. Or you can choose to apply the truth of God's word and experience freedom by shifting your thinking.

The Holy Spirit will guide you. The Holy Spirit will speak the truth to you and help you overcome your challenges. The Holy Spirit will prompt you, nudge you, and guide you in ALL things. God is not the author of confusion. God does not give us anxiety. When you yield to the Holy Spirit you have access to wisdom, discernment, truth, peace, and comfort. However, you cannot lean into the Holy Spirit and choose God's way with a disordered mind. Remember, a doubleminded person is unstable in all their ways.

The Holy Spirit is not here to make you dance and shout. It may be wonderful to experience His presence in that way, but that is not His ultimate purpose. The Holy Spirit is God. The Holy Spirit is the genius mind of Christ. The Holy Spirit gives you peace, clarity, purpose, and instructions. He unfolds the mysteries of God, guides you in trouble, strengthens you in weakness and can become your best friend and confidant. You live at an ADVANTAGE when you allow the Holy Spirit to actively participate in your life.

When you are burdened with the cares of the world, living in fear, baffled, and confused, it is because you are not connected to the Holy Spirit. You are not in fellowship with Him. You are not inviting Him into the affairs of your life. It is like having a wonderful friend on the other side of the door whom you do not invite in.

When you order your thinking, you will become more sensitive and aware of the Holy Spirit speaking to you. With a renewed mind you can tap into the DNA of God and participate in the divine nature. You are no longer a victim who is susceptible to the gloom and doom of every news source, and all of life's problems. You are no longer in bondage to fear and anxiety.

In *Living with the Advantage*, Dr. Corletta Vaughn writes, "Your mind is used to calling the shots, it's used to directing you. Most of your life you have lived by your soul, your emotions, and your will. The ultimate purpose of the Holy Spirit is to transform you. To rearrange things in you." (p.60) The Holy Spirit's assignment is to transform you into the image of Christ.

You have the advantage. You do not have to live a life of fear, lack, or be overcome by the undue challenges life brings. The Holy Spirit that raised Jesus from the dead lives in you (Romans 8:11). You have a resident healer, deliverer, provider, comforter, and as the old folks used to say, a heart fixer and a mind regulator.

Since the Spirit of God dwells in you, when you cultivate that relationship, the Holy Spirit has a powerful influence over your thoughts and choices. Not only will the Holy Spirit order your steps, but the Holy Spirit also has the power to overcome your mindset. When you are caught in a difficult situation, and your mind is spinning out of control, shift your thinking to the things that are lovely, good, and praiseworthy. Worship and magnify God for His spotless character and nature because it never changes. In doing so, you will create space for the Holy Spirit to speak – to guide you, to comfort you, to give you peace. When you choose life with the Holy

Spirit, you choose to live with the advantage. When you choose life with the Holy Spirit, you will be in awe of God.

Prayer

Holy Spirit, it is my desire to live with the advantage of your presence, power, and direction. Forgive me for my ignorance of who you are and the role you desire to play in my life. I invite you in and will trust your ways. As I seek you more, take control of my thoughts and my responses to the world around me. Amen.

Works Cited

Brueggemann, Walter. *Delivered out of Empire.* Westminster John Knox Press, 2021.

Diga Hernandez, David. *Holy Spirit Bondage Breaker.* Destiny Image Publishers, 2023

Kinde, Christa. *Managing Your Emotions.* Restore & Renew Bible Studies, Thomas Nelson, 2004.

Moser, Lance. *Clouded by Emotion: Studies on the Holy Spirit and Miracles.* Lance Mothe, 2019.

Munroe, Myles. *The Most Important Person on Earth: The Holy Spirit, Governor of the Kingdom.* Whitaker House, 2007.

Philips, Anita. *The Garden Within.* Anita L. Philips, 2023.

Scazzero, Peter. *Emotionally Healthy Spirituality: It's Impossible to Be Spiritually Mature, While Remaining Emotionally Immature.* Zondervan, 2017.

Vaughn, Corletta, *Living with the Advantage*, Corletta J. Vaughn, 2021.

Watchman Nee. *The Spiritual Man.*, Living Stream Ministry, 1998.

WEBSITES

Cherry, Kendra. "The Purpose of Emotions." *Very Well Mind*, 17 May 2020, www.verywellmind.com/the-purpose-of-emotions-2795181.Accessed 25 April 2024.

Sunshyne. "5 Ways to Manage Your Emotions." *Christian Counseling*, 9 July 2018,

www.sunsynegray.com/5-ways-to=mange-your-emotions/. Accessed 4 May 2024.

Aiyegbusi, Segun, "Identifying the Strongholds in Your Life (5 Areas to Consider)." 24 April 2024,

www.shegznstuff.com/blogofshegz/identifyingstrongholds?rq=strongholds.Accessed 25 April 2024.

www.ingramcontent.com/pod-product-compliance
Lightning Source LLC
Chambersburg PA
CBHW061348040426
42444CB00011B/3140